First World War
and Army of Occupation
War Diary
France, Belgium and Germany

2 DIVISION
2 Light Brigade
Headquarters
6 April 1919 - 25 October 1919

WO95/1374/5

The Naval & Military Press Ltd
www.nmarchive.com
Published in association with The National Archives

Published by

The Naval & Military Press Ltd

Unit 10 Ridgewood Industrial Park,

Uckfield, East Sussex,

TN22 5QE England

Tel: +44 (0) 1825 749494

www.naval-military-press.com

www.nmarchive.com

This diary has been reprinted in facsimile from the original. Any imperfections are inevitably reproduced and the quality may fall short of modern type and cartographic standards.

© **Crown Copyright**
Images reproduced by permission of The National Archives, London, England, 2015.

Contents

Document type	Place/Title	Date From	Date To
Heading	WO95/1374/5		
Heading	2 Division HQ 2 Light Brigade 1919 April-1919 Oct		
War Diary	Gill	06/04/1919	31/05/1919
Miscellaneous	2nd Light Brigade Special Order	17/05/1919	17/05/1919
Miscellaneous	Warning Order 2nd Light Brigade Order No.2	23/05/1919	23/05/1919
Miscellaneous	Guards Found By 1st Northern Brigade		
Miscellaneous	Guards Found By 3rd Northern Brigade		
Miscellaneous	2nd Light Brigade	26/05/1919	26/05/1919
Miscellaneous	Table A		
Miscellaneous	Table B Guards Found By 1st Northern Brigade		
Miscellaneous	Guards Found By 3rd Northern Brigade		
War Diary		01/06/1919	30/06/1919
Miscellaneous	Warning Order 2nd Light Brigade Order No.2	23/05/1919	23/05/1919
Miscellaneous	Guards Found By 1st Northern Brigade		
Miscellaneous	Guards Found By 3rd Northern Brigade		
Miscellaneous	2nd Light Brigade O.P.2	30/05/1919	30/05/1919
Miscellaneous	2nd Light Brigade O.P.4	22/06/1919	22/06/1919
Miscellaneous	2nd Light Brigade C.P./B.	24/06/1919	24/06/1919
Miscellaneous	2nd Light Brigade Ref. No. Cp/6	29/06/1919	29/06/1919
War Diary		01/07/1919	31/07/1919
Operation(al) Order(s)	2nd Light Brigade Order No.3	06/07/1919	06/07/1919
Miscellaneous	2nd Light Brigade Ref. No.A 20/5/2	07/07/1919	07/07/1919
Miscellaneous	2nd Light Brigade Ref. No.A 20/5		
Miscellaneous	2nd Light Brigade O.P/5	24/06/1919	24/06/1919
War Diary		01/08/1919	31/08/1919
War Diary	Ohligs	01/10/1919	25/10/1919
Operation(al) Order(s)	2nd Light Brigade Order No. O.P.12/5	13/10/1919	13/10/1919
Miscellaneous	2nd Light Brigade No. O.P.18/6/2	20/10/1919	20/10/1919
Miscellaneous	2nd Light Brigade No. O.P.12/6/1		
Miscellaneous	2nd Light Brigade No. O.P.12/6/3	21/10/1919	21/10/1919
Miscellaneous	Moves in Connection With Reduction of 6th And 9th London Regiments		

WO 95/13745

2 (~~LIGHT~~) DIVISION

HQ 2 LIGHT BRIGADE

1919 APRIL — 1919 OCT

WAR DIARY
or
INTELLIGENCE SUMMARY.

(Erase heading not required.)

Army Form C. 2118.

Place	Date	Hour	Summary of Events and Information	Remarks and references to Appendices
GILL	APRIL 6-30.		**2nd LIGHT BRIGADE.**	
			1. At 06.00 hours on April 6th, the 99th Infantry Brigade became the 2nd Light Brigade.	
			2. On the 6th, the 5th Royal Irish Regt. left the Brigade to become the Light Division Pioneer Battalion. The 6th Battn. London Regt. marched from the ZONS area and were accomodated in billets at NETTESHEIM, BUTZHEIM, ECKUM, ANSTEL, the move being complete at 15.00 hours.	
			On the 7th, the 18th K.R.R.C. left the Brigade and marched to DORMAGEN to join the 1st Light Brigade. The 9th Battn. London Regt. arrived at ROMMERSKIRCHEN station and marched to billets in NIEDERAUSSEM and OBERAUSSEM.	
			On the 8th, the 51st Rifle Brigade left the 2nd Light Brigade and marched to join the 3rd. The 12th Battn. Royal Irish Rifles arrived at ROMMERSKIRCHEN station and marched to billets at STOMMELN.	
			On the 17th, the 2nd Machine Gun Battalion was transferred from the 1st Light Brigade Group to the 2nd Light Brigade Group.	
			On the 18th, the 1st K.R.R.C. (Cadre) moved from BUSDORF to FLIESTEDEN, remaining in the Brigade Group.	
			The Brigade Group was now finally reconstituted; and Units were distributed as follows:-	
			Brigade Headquarters GILL	
			12th Battn. R.I.Rifles. STOMMELN	
			6th Battn. London Regt. NETTESHEIM, BUTZHEIM, ECKUM, ANSTEL.	
			9th Battn. London Regt. NIEDERAUSSEM, OBERAUSSEM	
			1st K.R.R.C. (Cadre) FLIESTEDEN	
			2nd Light T.M. Battery. GROSSMONCHHOF	
			2nd Machine Gun Battalion. EVINGHOVEN	
			483 Bd. Coy. R. E. VANIKUM	
			100th Field Ambulance. GLESSEN	
			No. 2 Coy Train. RHELT.	

Army Form C. 2118.

WAR DIARY
or
INTELLIGENCE SUMMARY
(Erase heading not required.)

Instructions regarding War Diaries and Intelligence Summaries are contained in F. S. Regs., Part II. and the Staff Manual respectively. Title pages will be prepared in manuscript.

Place	Date	Hour	Summary of Events and Information	Remarks and references to Appendices
			-2-	
			3. Throughout the month, the work of reorganization was carried on; and the General Officer Commanding visited and inspected the various units, and held Conferences of Commanding Officers at Brigade Headquarters (on the 10th and 22nd)	
			4. The Divisional Commander inspected the 9th Battn. London Regt. on the 25th and the 6th Battn. London Regt. on the 30th, and held a Conference of the Brigade Commanders of the Division on the 19th at the Headquarters of the 2nd Light Brigade.	
			5. On the 17th, Lieut. W.H. BRASHER, 6th Battn. London Regt. arrived at Brigade Headquarters to take up the duties of Assistant Staff Captain. On the 19th, Lieut. J.L. HENDERSON, Light Division Signal Co., took over the duties of Signal Officer. Captain T. COULSON, 12th Battn. Royal Irish Rifles, arrived on the 22nd and took over the duties of Brigade Gas Officer; and on the 23rd Lieut R.E. SCOTT, M.C. 12th Battn. Royal Irish Rifles, took up the duties of Sports Officer.	

A. Munir
Brigadier General,
Commanding 2nd Light Brigade.

Army Form C. 2118.

WAR DIARY
or
INTELLIGENCE SUMMARY.
(Erase heading not required.)

Instructions regarding War Diaries and Intelligence Summaries are contained in F. S. Regs., Part II. and the Staff Manual respectively. Title pages will be prepared in manuscript.

Place	Date	Hour	Summary of Events and Information	Remarks and references to Appendices
GILL	MAY. 1-5		2nd LIGHT BRIGADE.	
			The distribution of the various Units remained unchanged.	
			Brigade Headquarters GILL	
			12th R.I.Rifles STOMMELN	
			6th London Regt. NETTESHEIM-BUTZHEIM-	
			ECKUM-ANSTEL	
			9th London Regt. NIMBERAUSSEM-OBERAUSSEM	
			1st K.R.R.C.(Cadre) FLIESTEDEN	
			2nd M.G. Battn. EVINGHOVEN	
			2nd Light T.M. Battery. Gross MONCHOF.	
			483rd Field Company R.E. VANIKUM.	
			100th Field Ambulance. GLESSEN.	
			No 2 Company Train. RHEIDT.	
	5-11		On the 5th a Conference of all Commanding Officers was held at Brigade Headquarters. The Divisional Commander inspected the 12th R.I.Rifles at STOMMELN on May 7th. Inspections of billets of 6th London Regt and 12th R.I.Rifles were carried out during this period by the Brigadier General Commanding.	
	12-17		During this period individual training was carried out. On the 17th at 09.40 hours Sir William ROBERTSON, G.C.B. K.C.V.O. D.S.O. A.D.C. Commander-in-Chief, British Army of the Rhine, inspected the Brigade at RHEIDT. The Commander-in-Chief expressed his satisfaction and at his request the Brigadier General Commanding issued a Special Order of the Day (marked "A" and attached).	
	18-20		The training of the Brigade was uninterrupted during this period, the only incident of note was the Conference of Brigade Commanders held at 2nd Light Brigade Headquarters by the Divisional Commander.	

Army Form C. 2118.

WAR DIARY
or
INTELLIGENCE SUMMARY.

Instructions regarding War Diaries and Intelligence Summaries are contained in F. S. Regs., Part II. and the Staff Manual respectively. Title pages will be prepared in manuscript.

Place	Date	Hour	Summary of Events and Information	Remarks and references to Appendices
	MAY ~~APRIL~~ 21-31			

On the 21st the Brigade was warned that in case of an advance it would be called upon to Garrison COLOGNE and take over all Guards in that town.
On the 23rd Battalion Commanders visited COLOGNE making a reconnaissance of th areas which they were to take over from the Brigades of the NORTHERN DIVISION.
The succeeding days were uneventful.

Changes (1) Units.

On the 14th the Cadre of the 1st K.R.R.C. left the Brigade, entraining at ROMMERSKIRCHEN.STA.
The 100th Field Ambulance ceased to operate on the 24th, in process of reduction to cadre,
The 5th Field Ambulance now serves the Brigade.

(2) Personal.

On the 21st Capt. A.I. ELLIS proceeded to Demobilization Camp at COLOGNE and the duties of Brigade Education Officer were taken over by Capt. A.W. ELLIOTT. M.C. Bedfordshire Regt.
Capt. T. COULSON, Brigade Gas Officer, left the Brigade to take up an appointment as Chemical Adviser at G. H. Q.

Weather

Throughout the month the weather was ideal for training.

Construction.

Rapid progress was made with the rifle range at STOMMELN and the smaller 30 yards ranges in the Unit Areas.
Much work was done in the improvement of billets and Dining Halls.

Army Form C. 2118.

WAR DIARY
or
INTELLIGENCE SUMMARY.
(Erase heading not required.)

Place	Date	Hour	Summary of Events and Information	Remarks and references to Appendices
	MAY 4TH		-3- **Sports and Amusements.** During the month cricket replaced football and before the end of the month every Unit had a regimental team in existence and had played at least one inter-regimental match. Cinemas and concert parties were formed by Battalions and exchanges by Units enabled men of the different Units, although some distance apart, to hear or see the effort of other Battalions. 4/6/1919. W Rhodes Lieut-Colonel, Commanding 2nd Light Brigade.	

"A"

2nd LIGHT BRIGADE.

SPECIAL ORDER.

The Commander-in-Chief has requested me to express to every Officer, N.C.O and man of the 2nd Light Brigade his personal appreciation of the soldierlike manner in which to-day's parade for his inspection was carried out.

He was very favourably impressed by the smartness and turnout of all ranks, by their steadiness on parade, and by the precision with which both the troops and the transport marched past him.

The result reflects great credit on all concerned, and I look to each Battalion in the Brigade to do its utmost, not only to maintain but to improve upon, the reputation it has gained to-day.

The 2nd Light Brigade has not long been formed, but it has started well. I feel confident that all ranks, by their soldierly bearing both on and off parade, by the zeal and energy with which they enter into their training and their games, and by a high sense of esprit de corps and good comradeship, will in the future aim at producing a higher standard of all round military efficiency than can be found in any other formation of the British Army of the Rhine.

May 17th, 1919.

Brigadier General,
Commanding 2nd Light Brigade.

SECRET.

Copy No......

23rd May, 1919.

WARNING ORDER.
2ND. LIGHT BRIGADE ORDER NO.2.

1. The 2nd.Light Brigade Group is to be prepared to move to the COLOGNE area in accordance with paragraph 2 below, and to relieve guards at present being furnished by the Northern Division.

2. (a) 12th.R.I.Rifles are to be prepared to move by road or lorries at short notice on the 24th.instant to take over the guards at present found by the 1st.and 2nd.Northern Brigades.
   Details of these guards are shewn in the attached Appendix.

   (b) Two Companies, 9th.London Regiment, will be prepared to move on the 24th.instant at short notice to take over the guards at present found by 3rd.Northern Brigade (see Appendix attached).

   (c) The following Units will be prepared to move by road or lorries on the 25th.instant:-

   Brigade Headquarters.
   6th.London Regiment.
   9th.London Regiment (less 2 Companies)
   2nd.Light T.M.B.
   100th.Field Ambulance.
   483rd.Field Coy.R.E.
   No.2 Coy.Train.

3. If the move takes place, Units will move complete with all personnel and baggage as for a change of station.
   Troops will move in Battle Order, lorries being provided for packs.
   Instructions as to disposal of barrack furniture, paillasses, etc., will be issued later.

4. The present Light Divisional area will continue to be administered as at present. The Civil Staff Captain will therefore not move with a Brigade, but will remain behind to administer this area.

5. Full details as to embussing and debussing points (if any) and billeting areas will be issued as soon as known.
   ACKNOWLEDGE.

   W.Brackin
   Captain,
   A/Brigade Major,
   2nd.Light Brigade.

Issued through Signals at 08.00 hrs. to:-

```
Copy No.  1   to 12th.R.I.Rifles.
          2      6th.London Regt.
          3      9th.London Regt.
          4      2nd.L.T.M.B.
          5      100th.Field Ambulance
          6      483rd.Field Coy.R.E.
          7      No.2 Coy.Train.
          8      Light Division "G"
          9      Light Division "Q"
         10.     G.O.C.
         11.     P.H.
         12.     S.C.
         13.     Signal Officer
         14.     Civil Staff Captain.
         15.     War Diary
         16.     H.Q.Light Div.Train.
         17.     File.
```

GUARDS FOUND BY 1ST. NORTHERN BRIGADE

		Offrs.	NCO's.	Pten.
1.	Docks, MARIENBURG. (1 Company)	3.	10.	77.
2.	SCHFUR GASSE. (Detention Barracks)		2.	8.
3.	Powder Magazine. RADERBERG. (1 Company).	4.	10.	70.
4.	Fort VII. (1 Platoon)	2.	5.	28.
5.	BONN Tor Goods Station.		2.	8.
6.	Train Guard. (Docks to Eiffel Tor)		3.	94.
7.	C. in C's House, MARIENBURG.		2.	30.
8.	MARIENBURG Supply Depot. Eiffel Tor Goods Station.	1.	4.	41.
9.	2nd. Army Troops M.T.COY. Altenburg Brewery, MARIENBURG.		2.	8.
		10.	40.	364.

GUARDS FOUND BY 2ND. NORTHERN BRIGADE

		Offrs.	NCO's.	Pten.
1.	Nippes Artillery Depot (1 Company).	4	20	120
2.	M.T. Depot. EHRENFELD.		2.	12
3.	Pichendorf Bakery, EHRENFELD.		2	6
4.	Naarwig R.E. Dump. BRAUNSFELD.		1	7
5.	Subblorather Strasse (Arm)		1	3
6.	Police Prasidium (NEUMARKT)		2	2
		4	28	150

GUARDS FOUND BY 3RD. NORTHERN BRIGADE.

		Offrs.	NCO's.	Ptes.
1.	MULHEIM BRIDGE.	1	4	20
2.	M.C's House.		2	8
3.	Wireless Station, (RIEHL)		2	9
4.	Refilling Point. (NEHHL)		2	4
5.	MONOPOL GROUP (1 Company)	5	10	65
6.	Arsenal.	1	5	29 *
7.	M.C's Office, (MONOPOL)		2	9
		5	27	144

* Includes 2 Cooks and 2 Signallers.

	Offrs	NCO's	Ptes
1st. Northern Brigade................	10	40	284
2nd. Northern Brigade................	4	28	150
3rd. Northern Brigade................	5	27	144
	19	95	578

NOTE. If necessary the above guards may be reduced so as
to allow sentries to have 2 hours on and 4 hours off.
This adjustment can of course be made only after the
guards have been taken over.

SECRET.

To:- 12th Battn. R.I.Rifles.   2nd Light Brigade.
    6th Battn. London Regt.
    9th Battn. London Regt.
    2nd Light T.M. Battery.
    100th Field Ambulance. 483rd Fd Coy. R.E.
    No 2 Company Train.
    Light Division (2).   )
    1st Northern Brigade.) for information.
    2nd   "   "   )
    3rd   "   "   )

1.   In the event of orders being received to take over Guards of the Northern Division forecast in 2nd Light Brigade Warning Order No 2 dated May 23rd, moves and reliefs will take place in accordance with the attached Tables A and B. Table B shows an amended list of Guards to be relieved.

2.   The 100th Field Ambulance will not move.

3.   Troops will move in battle order, lorries being provided for packs. Those troops moving by bus or lorry will carry their packs and take their Lewis Guns and 8 drums per gun with them.

4.   All defence schemes and Guard orders will be taken over.

Units of Brigade Group to acknowledge.

                                G. Whittuck, Captain.
                                    Brigade Major.
26/5/1919.   2nd Light Brigade.

Copies to:- Light Divisional Train.
            Brigade Signal Officer.
            Civil Staff Captain.

TABLE A.

UNIT	STRENGTH	DATE	FROM	TO	IN RELIEF OF	MOVE BY LORRY	MOVE BY MARCH	REMARKS.
12 R.I.R.	2 Coys	J-3	STOMMELN	RIEHL B'KS		?	STOMMELN 0800 hrs	If lorries are available they will be at STOMMELN 0800 hours
	2 Coys	J-2	RIEHL B'KS	Relieve Guards of 2nd N'THN Bde RIEHL-MULHEIM-COLOGNE Area				
	H.Qrs & 2 Coys	J-2	STOMMELN	Camp BICKENDORF			STOMMELN 0800 hrs	
	H.Qrs & 2 Coys	J-1	BICKENDORF	RIEHL B'CKS	Billets from Staff Capt.,		0800 hrs	
6 Ldn.	2 Coys	J-3	NETTESHEIM	NIPPES Area	Guards 2nd N'thn Bde NIPPES-EHRENFELD, COLOGNE Area	PUTZ-HEIM 0900 (200 men)		Guides from 2nd Northern Brigade Busses in centre of BICKENDORF at 1000 hrs. Transport proceed direct to School HARTWIG STRASSE NIPPES.
	H.Qrs & 2 Coys	J-3	NETTESHEIM	PULHEIM	Billets from Staff Capt.,		NETTES-HEIM 1000 hrs	
	H.Qrs & 2 Coys	J-2	PULHEIM	NIPPES Area HARTWIG STRASSE School			PULHEIM 0800 hrs	

TABLE 7 (cont'd)

UNIT	STRENGTH	DATE	FROM	TO	IN RELIEF OF	HOUR OF FIRST MARCH	REMARKS
9 Lan.	2 Coys.	J-3	MIEDRAUSSEM	ARTILLERY B'CKS MARIEMBURG		NIEDRAUSSEM 0900 hours	Transport direct to Artillery B'ks
	2 Coys.	J-2	Artillery B'ks To relieve guards of 1st B'thn Bde.,MARIEMBURG— RADEBURG Area		(350 men)		Coys.to remain Artillery B'ks
	H.Cys & 2 Coys	J-2	NIEDRAUSSEM	Camp,BICKENDORF		NIEDER-AUSSEM 0800 hrs	
	H.Cys & 2 Coys	J-1	BICKENDORF	VIEHL BARRACKS	Billets from Staff Capt.	0915 hrs	
	2 Coys	J+2	Guards MARIEMBURG— RADEBURG Area	VIEHL BARRACKS			Relieved by 1st Light Brigade.
2nd Light Bde H.Cys		J-3	GILL	POULHEIM	Billets from Staff Capt.,	1600 hrs	
		J-2	POULHEIM	Camp BICKEN-DORF		0900 hrs	
		J-1	BICKENDORF	57 HOHENSTRAUFEN RING	3rd B'thn Bde.	0800 hrs 0330	
2nd L.T.M.B.		J-3	MONCHOF FARM	POULHEIM		1800 hrs	
		J-2	POULHEIM	Camp,BICKENDORF		0910 hrs	
		J-1	BICKENDORF	VIEHL BARRACKS	Billets from Staff Capt.,	1000 hrs.	

TABLE A (Contd)

UNIT	STRENGTH	DATE	FROM	TO	IN RELIEF OF	MOVE BY LORRY MARCH	REMARKS
483rd Co.R.E.		3-2 3-1	MAHLEM EICKENDORF	Camp. EICKENDORF Entrance to FLORAGARTEN-RIEHL	38 Fd. Coy. R.E.	0700 hrs 0935 hrs	
No.2Coy.Train.		3-2 3-1	RHEIN EICKENDORF	Camp. EICKENDORF RIEHL BARRACKS	Billets from Staff-Capt.,	0300 hrs 1015 hrs	

TABLE B.

GUARDS FOUND BY 1ST. NORTHERN BRIGADE.

		Off.	NCO's	Ptes.
1.	Docks, MARIENBURG. (1 Company)	3	12	73
2.	SCHNUR GASSE. (Detention Barracks)		2	8
3.	Powder Magazine. RADERBURG (1 Coy)	4	10	70
4.	Fort VII. (1 Platoon).	2	3	22
5.	Train Guard. (Docks to Eiffel Tor)		3	24
6.	C-I-C's House, MARIENBERG. (3rd M.G.Bn)		2	14
7.	MARIENBURG Supply Depot. Eiffel Tor Goods Station.	1	4	41
8.	2nd Army Troops M.T. Coy. Attenburg Brewery, MARIENBURG		2	8
9.	I.F.C. Depot. BAYERNSTRASSE. Cotton Spinnery		1	6
10.	44 Casualty Clearing Station.(UBIERRING)		2	10
11.	Militar Lazarette Kartauser Wall Ordnance Depot.		1	6
		10	42	282

GUARDS FOUND BY 2ND. NORTHERN BRIGADE.

1.	NIPPES Artillery Depot.(1 Company)	4	20	120
2.	M.T. Depot. EHRENFELD.		2	12
3.	Ordnance Clothing Depot. HANDESTRASSE.		2	12
4.	Bubblerather Strasse (Amm)		1	3
5.	Police Prasidium. (NEUMARKT)		2	6
		4	27	153

GUARDS FOUND BY 3RD NORTHERN BRIGADE.

		Offs.	NCOS	PTES	
1.	MULHEIM BRIDGE.	1	4	20	
2.	M.G's House.		2	8	
3.	Wireless Station (RIEHL)		2	9	
4.	Refilling Point. (RIEHL)		2	4	
5.	MONOPOL GROUP (1 Company)	3	10	65	
6.	Arsenal.	1	5	29	x
7.	M.G's Office (MONOPOL) 9th (P) Bn. DURHAM L.I.	(	2	9	
		(	1	9	ø
		5	28	153	

x Includes 2 Cooks and 2 Signallers.

ø Orderlies and Cooks.

1st Northern Brigade.	10	42	282
2nd " "	4	27	153
3rd " "	5	28	153
	19	97	588

NOTE If necessary the above guards may be reduced so as to allow sentries to have 2 hours on and 4 hours off. This adjustment can of course be made only after the guards have been taken over.

Army Form C. 2118.

WAR DIARY
or
INTELLIGENCE SUMMARY

(Erase heading not required)

Summary of Events and Information
2nd LIGHT BRIGADE

Place	Date	Hour	Summary of Events and Information	Remarks and references to Appendices
	JUNE. 1-2		The Battalions of the Brigade commenced Platoon Training.	
	3		The King's Birthday. Each Battalion held a ceremonial parade at which the Royal Salute was given. Sports were held in the afternoon. The G.O.C. left for England on leave and Lt. Col. GOODWIN, C.M.G., D.S.O., assumed command of the Brigade.	
	4-15.		Training under normal conditions continued, except that the 9th, Whit Monday, was a holiday. The Corps Commander visited all Units on the 13th and inspected billets and accomodation.	
	16		Warning Order received that the Brigade might be required to move to COLOGNE for Garrison Duty.	
	17		Order to move received at 0800 hours. This day now became J-3 day of O.P. No. 1 attached. All movements of troops were as per programme.	
	18		J-2 day. Movement of troops conformed to programme.	
	19.		J-1 day. The movement of troops conformed to programme. Brigade H.Q. opened at 57, HOHENSTAUFEN RING, COLOGNE.	
	20		J day. The Units of the Brigade were now employed finding Guards and "standing by" in emergency stations. Brigadier General R. A. CURRIE, C.M.G., D.S.O., returned from leave and Lt. Col. R. W. GOODWIN, C.M.G., D.S.O., rejoined the 12th Royal Irish Rifles.	
	21		The 18th Bn. K.R.R.C. arrived at MARIENBERG Barracks and came under the order of G.O.C. 2nd Light Brigade.	
	22		18th Bn. K.R.R.C. took over Dock Guards of the 9th London Regiment.	
	23-27		Battalions continued to furnish Guards.	
	28		PEACE was signed.	

Army Form C. 2118.

WAR DIARY
or
INTELLIGENCE SUMMARY.
(Erase heading not required.)

Instructions regarding War Diaries and Intelligence Summaries are contained in F. S. Regs., Part II. and the Staff Manual respectively. Title pages will be prepared in manuscript.

Place	Date	Hour	Summary of Events and Information	Remarks and references to Appendices
	29		The Order to return to GILL area was received. Movement of troops was in accordance with C.P. 5 (attached). The day was A-1 day of C.P.5.	
	30		All Guards were relieved in accordance with O.Ps. No. 5 & 6.	
			Brigade Headquarters Strength :- 6 Officers 119 Other Ranks. Copy of C.P. 1 was forwarded with War Diary for month of May.	

July 5th, 1919.

[signature]
Brigadier General,
Commanding 2nd Light Brigade.

SECRET.

Copy No......

23rd May, 1919.

WARNING ORDER.

2ND. LIGHT BRIGADE ORDER NO.2.

1. The 2nd.Light Brigade Group is to be prepared to move to the COLOGNE area in accordance with paragraph 2 below, and to relieve guards at present being furnished by the Northern Division.

2. (a) 12th.R.I.Rifles are to be prepared to move by road or lorries at short notice on the 24th.instant to take over the guards at present found by the 1st.and 2nd.Northern Brigades. Details of these guards are shewn in the attached Appendix.

   (b) Two Companies, 9th.London Regiment, will be prepared to move on the 24th.instant at short notice to take over the guards at present found by 3rd.Northern Brigade (see Appendix attached).

   (c) The following Units will be prepared to move by road or lorries on the 25th.instant:-

   Brigade Headquarters.
   6th.London Regiment.
   9th.London Regiment (less 2 Companies)
   2nd.Light T.M.B.
   100th.Field Ambulance.
   483rd.Field Coy.R.E.
   No.2 Coy.Train.

3. If the move takes place, Units will move complete with all personnel and baggage as for a change of station.
   Troops will move in Battle Order, lorries being provided for packs.
   Instructions as to disposal of barrack furniture, paillasses,etc., will be issued later.

4. The present Light Divisional area will continue to be administered as at present. The Civil Staff Captain will therefore not move with a Brigade, but will remain behind to administer this area.

5. Full details as to embussing and debussing points (if any) and billeting areas will be issued as soon as known.
   ACKNOWLEDGE.

Captain,
A/Brigade Major,
2nd.Light Brigade.

Issued through Signals at 08.00 hrs. to:-

```
Copy No.  1   to 12th.R.I.Rifles.
          2      6th.London Regt.
          3      9th.London Regt.
          4      2nd.L.T.M.B.
          5      100th.Field Ambulance
          6      483rd.Field Coy.R.E.
          7      No.2 Coy.Train.
          8      Light Division "G"
          9      Light Division "Q"
         10.     G.O.C.
         11.     B.M.
         12.     S.C.
         13.     Signal Officer
         14.     Civil Staff Captain.
         15.     War Diary
         16.     H.Q.Light Div.Train.
         17.     File.
```

GUARDS FOUND BY 1ST. NORTHERN BRIGADE

		Offrs.	NCO's.	Rten.
1.	Docks, MARIENBURG. (1 Company)	3.	12.	75.
2.	SCHNUR GASSE. (Detention Barracks)		2.	8.
3.	Powder Magazine. BADENBERG. (1 Company).	4.	10.	70.
4.	Fort VII. (1 Platoon)	2.	5.	22.
5.	BOBT Tor Goods Station.		2.	8.
6.	Train Guard. (Docks to Eiffel Tor)		2.	24.
7.	C.in C's House, MARIENBERG.		2.	30.
8.	MARIENBURG Supply Depot. Eiffel Tor Goods Station.	1.	4.	41.
9.	2nd.Army Troops M.T.COY. Attenburg Brewery,MARIENBURG.		2.	8.
		10.	40.	284.

GUARDS FOUND BY 2ND. NORTHERN BRIGADE

1.	Nippes Artillery Depot (1 Company).	4	20	120
2.	M.T.Depot. EHRENFELD.		2.	12
3.	Bichendorf Bakery, EHRENFELD.		2	6
4.	Naarwig R.E. Dump. BRAUNSFELD.		1	5
5.	Subblorather Strasse (Arm)		1	3
6.	Police Prasidium (NEUMARKT)		2	6
		4	28	150

GUARDS FOUND BY 3RD. NORTHERN BRIGADE.

		Offrs.	NCO's.	Ptes.
1.	MULHEIM BRIDGE.	1	2	20
2.	M.G's House.		2	8
3.	Wireless Station, (RIEHL)		2	9
4.	Refilling Point. (REEHL)		2	4
5.	MONOPOL GROUP (1 Company)	3	10	65
6.	Arsenal.	1	7	29.*
7.	M.G's Office,, MONOPOL)		2	9
		5	27	144

* Includes 2 Cooks and 2 Signallers.

	Offrs	NCO's	Ptes
1st. Northern Brigade..................	10	40	284
2nd. Northern Brigade..................	4	28	150
3rd. Northern Brigade..................	5	27	144
	19	95	578
			673

NOTE. If necessary the above guards may be reduced so as to allow sentries to have 2 hours on and 4 hours off. This adjustment can of course be made only after the guards have been taken over.

SECRET.

To:- 12th Battn. R.I.Rifles.　　　　2nd Light Brigade. G.P.2.
　　　6th Battn. London Regt.
　　　9th Battn. London Regt.
　　　Brigade Supply Officer.
　　　Staff Captain.

1.　　　　The Ammunition supply system for the advanced Corps in the event of an advance involves composite Ammunition Trains being placed at ROMMERSKIRCHEN.

2.　　　　The first of these trains arrived from FRANCE on May 29th and will remain at ROMMERSKIRCHEN until required East of the RHINE.
　　　　6th Battn. London Regt. has supplied a guard of 1 officer and 20 men over this train.

3.　　　　As soon as the train moves on it will be replaced by another Ammunition train. Orders as to furnishing guard over this second train will be notified when the contingency arises.

4.　　　　6th Battn. London Regt. will be responsible for placing five days rations, water, tentage, fuel and light on the train for the use of the Guard if the train moves forward and at subsequent halts.
　　　　Four tents have been applied for from the Light Division. These tents will be taken on charge by 6th Battn. London Regt.
　　　　Rations, fuel and light will be drawn from the Brigade Supply Officer.
　　　　6th Battn. London Regt. will supply sufficient petrol tins for water.

5.　　　　Officer Commanding 6th Battn. London Regt. will issue the necessary written orders to the guard for the safety of the train including precautions against fire, method of guarding, and action in the event of the train moving forward.

6.　　　　The Guard will remain with the train until returned to FRANCE. Personnel will then rejoin their Battalion.

7.　　　　When the rations mentioned in para 4 are exhausted, the Officer in charge of the Guard will apply to the nearest Unit for rations, fuel and light.

　　　　　　　　　　　　　　　　　　　　　Captain.
　　　　　　　　　　　　　　　　　　　　　Brigade Major.
30/5/1919.　　　　　　　　　　　　　　　　2nd Light Brigade.

SECRET.

To:- 12th Battn. R.I. Rifles.   2nd Light Brigade. C.P.4.
     6th Battn. London Regt.
     9th Battn. London Regt.
     2nd Light T.M. Battery.
     483rd Field Coy. R.E.
     No 2 Company Train.
     100th Field Ambulance.
     18th K.R.R.C.
     2nd Machine Gun Battn.
     6th Field Ambulance.

ACTION TO BE TAKEN BY TROOPS OF 2nd LIGHT BRIGADE GROUP
IN THE EVENT OF CIVIL DISTURBANCES IN COLOGNE (PROVISIONAL).

1. **Minor Disturbance.**

   On receipt of code word "THAMES" from Brigade Headquarters by telephone or on the Alarm given by maroon or sounded by the bugler on any Guard :-

   (a) 18th K.R.R.C. will send two platoons to re-inforce the Guard at the Supply Depot of the Docks and 1 Company to 2nd Light Brigade Headquarters 57 HOHENSTAUFEN RING.

   (b) All remaining troops will stand by in their billets. Men in COLOGNE on hearing the "Alarm" will return at once to their unit parade ground.

   (c) The order to sound the "Alarm" will be given by any Staff Officer of the Army or Corps H.Q. or the Military Governor's Staff. Other buglers or guards will pick up the call and guards which have been provided with them will fire maroons. Buglers will step forward clear of the Guard Post, and sound the call in various directions.

   (d) Unit commanders will ensure all ranks are thoroughly acquainted with the "Alarm" sounded on the bugle and that buglers are able to sound the call quickly and well. They will be careful to prevent practice calls being taken for the genuine "Alarm".

   (e) All men will be continually warned on parade that in the case of disturbance or of crowds assembling they must keep clear, and not move in the direction of the crowds.

2. **Extensive Disturbances.**

   In the event of extensive civil disturbances being apprehended the following code messages will be sent out by Brigade Headquarters :-

   Warning Order .. .. "MOSELLE"
   Order to move .. .. "ERIN".

   (a) On the receipt of the code message "MOSELLE" :-

   (i) All troops will be at one hours notice.

   (ii) All officers will join and remain with their troops.

-2-

para 2
contd:
  (a) (iii) 12th R.I. Rifles will increase the garrison of MULHEIM Bridge to 2 platoons and O.C. 2nd Machine Gun Battn. will increase the Machine Gun Detachment there to one section.

    (iv) The patrolling of the railway between SUD Bridge and LUXEMBURG STRASSE (inclusive) by 6th London Regt and between LUXEMBURG STRASSE (exclusive) and KREFELDER STRASSE (inclusive) by 2nd Machine Gun Battn. will take place every four hours.

    (v) All Guards will be warned to be specially alert.

    (vi) Each unit will send an officer and 1 cycle orderly to 2nd Light Brigade Headquarters at once with list of exact strength of units available.

  (b) On receipt of the code message "RHINE":-

    (i) 9th Battn, London Regt (less 2 companies) will proceed to the DOM PLATZ and picquet all approaches to the railway station and the square. 18th K.R.R.C. will send one company to 2nd Light Brigade Headquarters 57 HOHENSTAUFFEN RING, 2 platoons to re-inforce the Guard at the Supply Depot at the Docks, and 2 platoons to Guard the Military Exchange, Central Telephone Exchange, CACILIEN STRASSE.

    (ii) The remaining troops of the 2nd Light Brigade Group (including 2nd Machine Gun Battn) will be in Divisional Reserve and remain in their present locations.

    (iii) An officer to be detailed from Brigade Headquarters and 6 cycle orderlies to be detailed by Brigade Signalling Officer will be sent at once to Northern Division H.Q.

3. General.

  (a) The Dress for all ranks will be fighting order. Lewis Guns will be taken by all re-inforcing units.

  (b) A Detachment of Tanks will probably cooperate with the Brigade Group.

  (c) Attention is called to the following points :-

    (i) Providing for security of transport lines.

    (ii) Providing for communication in the event of telephones being cut.

    (iii) Providing for lights in Headquarters if electric light is cut off.

4. ACKNOWLEDGE.

                                              Captain.
                                              Brigade Major.
                                              2nd Light Brigade.

22/6/1919.

Copies to:- G.O.C., S.C., Brigade Signal Officer.

SECRET.

To:- 12th Battn. R.I.Rifles.   2nd Light Brigade. C.R./3.
    6th Battn. London Regt.
    9th Battn. London Regt.
    2nd Machine Gun Battn.
    2nd Light T.M. Battery.
    483rd Field Coy. R.E.
    No 2 Company Train.
    18th K. R. R. C.
    6th Field Ambulance.
    Civil Staff Captain.
    Light Division.   )
    Light Division S.) for information.

1. In the event of the Division being ordered to move back to its normal area, the following warning instructions are issued.

2. On the day the order is received (A-1 Day) if not too late in the evening, one Battalion from each Infantry Brigade of the Northern Division will move by bus to COLOGNE.

On A Day guards found by 9th London Regt. and 18th K.R.R.C. will be relieved by "A" Battalion 1st Northern Brigade. Guards found by 6th London Regt by "A" Battalion 2nd Northern Brigade.

Guards found by 12th R.I.Rifles by "A" Battalion 3rd Northern Brigade.

3. On B Day the Brigade Group will proceed to SILL Area by bus.

The times and places of embussing will probably be as follows :-

Time	Unit	Place	Busses
09.00 hours.	6th London Regt.	PIUS STRASSE.head facing E at junction of VENLOER & PIUS STRASSE.	27 busses
09.00 hours.	9th London Regt.	RIEHL Infantry Barracks facing North	30 "
14.00 hours.	12th R.I.Rifles.	do	32 "
do	(Bde H.Qrs & 2nd (Light T.M.B.	do	6 "
do	1 Section 483rd Field Coy. R.E.	do	2 "
do	6th London Regt.	do	2 "
do	9th London Regt.	do	2 "

Lorries will be provided for stores. Dress - Marching Order. Lewis Guns and 8 drums per gun will be carried on busses.

4. Should the order be received so late on A-1 day that it is not possible for advanced Battalions of Northern Division to move into COLOGNE, relief of guards will take place on B Day and the move back to normal areas on C Day.

5. Transport will proceed direct by road. There will be no staging. Distances will be maintained on the march in accordance with G.H.Q. pamphlet on March Discipline. Time for march will be issued later.

6.   18th K. R. R. C. will proceed by boat to normal area, embarking near "U" Bridge on B Day (C Day if relief of guards is postponed).

7.   2nd Machine Gun Battn. will proceed to its normal area under orders received from Light Division.

8.   Please acknowledge.

24/6/19.

                                     Captain.
                                   Brigade Major.
                                   2nd Light Brigade.

SECRET

2nd. Light Brigade

Ref. No. Op/5.

12th. R.I. Rifles.
6th. London Regt.
9th. London Regt.
2nd. M.G. Bn.
2nd. Light T.M.B.
Section, 463rd. Field Coy. R.E. FLORA GARTEN.
No. 2 Coy. Train.
16th. K.R.R.C.
6th. Field Ambulance.
Civil Staff Captain.
Light Division.   ) For information.
Light Division, "Q")

Reference Map COLOGNE 1/200,000.

1. The reliefs and moves indicated in paras 2 & 3 of Warning Instructions - O.P/5/ of 24th. June, 1919, will be put into execution.

2. "A" Day will be Monday, June 30th.

3. Each Battalion will have guides for all their guards at their Battalion Headquarters (MARIENBURG Bks. in case of 9th. London Regt.) at 08.00 hours, June 30th. Details of relief will be arranged between C.O's concerned.
Reliefs will be carried out as follows:-

12th. R.I. Rifles. by 22nd. D.L.I. (quartered June 29/30 "C" Block, RIEHL Bks.)
6th. London Regt. by 1/5th. W. Yorks Regt. (quartered June 29/30 New School, SUBBELRATHER STRASSE, BICKENDORF).
9th. London Regt.)by 51st. Northnd. Fuslrs. (quartered June 29/30
16th. K.R.R.C.   )Schools, REDWITZ STRASSE) except for guard over C.-in-C's house, which will be relieved by 3rd. M.G. Bn.

Guards on relief will rejoin their Battalions. Detachment 9th. London Regt., at MARIENBURG will proceed to RIEHL on relief.

4. The following guards will not be relieved by Northern Division, and will be dismounted at the most convenient hour on June 30th.

Signal Centres found by 12th. R.I. Rifles.
SUBBELRATHER STRASSE found by 6th. London Regt.
Power Station, RIEHLTON, found by 9th. London Regt.

5. Receipts will be obtained for all articles on Guardroom inventory board. Maroons issued under 2nd. Light Brigade O.P./5 will be handed over upon relief.

6. Busses and lorries for the move on July 1st. will be as stated in O.P.5/5 of June 28th.
Special attention is called to G.R.O. 2877 re order for embussing and debussing.
17 Busses conveying 6th. London Regt. and all busses of 9th. London Regt., will return to RIEHL Bks. after the first journey to HETTERHEIM and NIEDERAUSSEM respectively with the exception of 2 detailed for 6th. London Regt., which will return to PIUS STRASSE School.
C's O., 6th. and 9th. London Regiments, will ensure that N.C.O's in charge of their respective bus columns are given these instructions and that they return to COLOGNE by 14.00 hours.

P.T.O

-2-

7. Lorries for stores may make a double journey. They must be despatched on the first journey by 07.00 hours.

8. Transport of units will proceed to normal areas by road on July 1st. Routes as desired.

No.2 Coy.Train.) 1 Section,423rd.) Field Coy.R.E.)	under O.C., 2 Coy.Train, not to pass ZOOLOGICAL GARDENS later than 03.00 hours.
6th.London Regt.	to pass Junction of VENLOER and BACHUS STRASSE at 08.30 hours.
9th.London Regt.	To be clear of RIEHL Bks. by 07.30 hours.
2nd.Light Bde.H.Q.) 2nd.Light T.M.B.)	under Brigade Education Officer, to clear RIEHL Bks. at 10.00 hours.
12th.R.I.Rifles.	Not to clear RIEHL Bks. before 11.00 hours.
18th.K.R.R.C.	To be clear of MARIENBURG Bks. by 08.00 hours.

9. A boat to convey dismounted personnel of 18th.K.R.R.C. to RHEINKASSEL will leave SHIP BRIDGE at 08.00 hours on July 1st. An Officer of I.W.T. will report to Officer Commanding,18th.K.R.R.C on the morning of June 30th. to arrange details. On embarking, 18th.K.R.R.C. revert to tactical command of O.C.G., 1st.Light Brigade.

10. The guard at Brigade Headquarters will be bussed to GILL under arrangements made by the Staff Captain.

11. Each unit will send a small advanced party to their normal areas by train, to-morrow, June 30th.

12. Officers commanding units will ensure that all Barracks, Billets and Guards are left clean and in good order.

13. Completion of reliefs of guards will be reported to Brigade Headquarters, by wire to-morrow, June 30th.
Arrival in normal areas will be reported to Brigade Headquarters at GILL.

14. 2nd.Light Brigade Headquarters will close at 27 Hohenstaufen Ring, at 14.30 hours, and open at the same hour at GILL.

G Whitsuck
Captain,
Brigade Major,
2nd.Light Brigade.

29/6/19.

Copy to Northern Division.

Army Form C. 2118.

WAR DIARY
or
INTELLIGENCE SUMMARY.
(Erase heading not required.)

Instructions regarding War Diaries and Intelligence Summaries are contained in F. S. Regs., Part II. and the Staff Manual respectively. Title pages will be prepared in manuscript.

Place	Date	Hour	Summary of Events and Information	Remarks and references to Appendices
	JULY. 1.		The Brigade moved back to the GILL Area by lorries. This day was the 'B' day of O.P. 5 & 6 (attached).	
	2-3.		Training was recommenced, and work continued on the Rifle Range at SPOTKULN.	
	4.		Warning order received that the Brigade might be called upon to relieve the 2nd.Lowland Brigade in the OHLIGS Area.	
	5.		Received orders to relieve 2nd. Lowland Brigade on the 8th. July.	
	6-7.		Normal. On the latter date an order was received postponing the move for 24 hours.	
	8.		Advance parties left for the forward area. Order No. 3, A./20/5/2, and A/20/6 are attached.	
	9.		Brigade moved to OHLIGS by train, thence by March route to the new Unit areas. New location as in para. 5 Order No. 3.	
	10-11.		Training recommenced in the new area. The G.O.C. visited the outpost line on both days.	
	12-18.		Training proceeded without interruption. On the 14th. and 15th. the G.O.C. inspected the billets of the 6th. and 9th. London Regts. respectively. Lt.P.P.C.FENNELL, 12th.P.I.Rifles, reported for duty as Assistant Staff Captain on the 17th.	
	19.		General Holiday.	
	20-22.		Training proceeded normally. On the 22nd. the Divisional Commander visited the outposts.	
	23.		General Holiday.	
	24-31.		Training proceeded without interruption. On the 28th. the 6th. London Regt. commenced their General Musketry Course on BRUCKERKOTTEN Range.	

August 6th. 1919.

Matthews Castor
for Brigadier-General,
Commanding 2nd.Light Bde.

SECRET.
Copy No:
6th. July, 1919.

2ND. LIGHT BRIGADE ORDER NO. 3.

Reference map Germany Sheet 2 K. 1/100,000.

1. The Light Division is to move to the BENRATH-OHLIGS-SOLINGEN Area, at present occupied by the Lowland Division, between July 8th. and 13th. the Lowland Division moving to the present Light Divisional Area.

2. The 2nd. Light Brigade Group-
    2nd. Light Brigade,
    1 Section 483rd. Field Coy. R.E.
    2 Company Light Divisional Train-

will move by train to the OHLIGS Area in relief of 2nd. Lowland Brigade on July 9th.
Details as to rail arrangements will be issued separately. Dress for entraining - Marching Order. Distances as laid down in Notes on March Discipline will be maintained on the march to and from entraining station.

3. A map showing 2nd. Lowland Brigade area is issued to Battalions, Trench Mortar Battery, and Brigade Signalling Officer.

4. 1 Lorry per Battalion and 1 Lorry for the remainder of the Brigade Group will take advance parties to the new area on July 8th. These parties will take rations with them for July 9th.
2nd. Lowland Brigade are sending advance parties to this area on July 8th. Units will arrange accommodation for these parties and hand over billets and explain training and range facilities and hutting schemes.

5. 2nd. Lowland Brigade Headquarters are at 89 WEYER OHLIGS.
On arrival in the new area, units will be located as follows:-

12th. R.I. Rifles.	31 Alter Kirchplatz. HAAN.	In relief of 11th. Royal Scots. (will also take over 2nd. Lowland Brigade School).
6th. London Regt.	KANZLER Hotel, OHLIGS.	In relief of 5/6th. Royal Scots.
9th. London Regt.	198 Kaiser Strasse, WALD.	In relief of 6th. K.O.S.B.
2nd. Light T.M.B.	School, KEMPER Strasse, WALD.	In relief of 2nd. Lowland T.M.B.
483rd. Field Coy. R.E.	181 Kaiser Strasse, WALD.	In relief of 90th. Field Coy. R.E.
No. 2 Coy. Train.	OHLIGS-SOLINGEN ROAD.	In relief of 3rd. Company Lowland Divisional Train.

Units of 2nd. Lowland Brigade move into the same accommodation in this area as occupied by relieving units of this Brigade

PTO

6. (a) Guards at Frontier Posts will be taken over in accordance with the following table.

Number and Name of Post	Approximate Location.	Found by	Relieved by	Strength N.C.Os.	Men.
No.1 Post KLUSE.	KLUSE.	6th K.O.S.B.	9th Ldn. Regt.	3	23
No.2 Post HOHE.	HOHE.	do	do	2	9
No.3 Post LOOP.	POLNMUTZE.	do	do	2	17
No.4 Post GRUITEN	¼ mile SS of BHF GRUITEN	11th Royal Scots	12th R.I.R.	2	6
No.5 Post RAILWAY	½ mile N E of ELP	do	do	2	6
No.6 Post ELP	ELP	do	do	Exact strength to be ascertained	
No.7 Post KELLERTHOR	KELLERTHOR	do	do	2	6

The above guards are at present found by 2 Coys 6th K.O.S.B. and 1 Coy 11th Royal Scots and will be relieved by 1 Coy 9th London Regt and 1 Coy 12th R.I.Rifles respectively.

(b) 6th London Regt. will take over the following guards from 5/6th Royal Scots.
OHLIGS STATION Control   4 Offrs. 4 N.C.Os. 20 men.
OHLIGS Railhead Guard   3   "   15 "

(c) The platoon and section organisation will be maintained in taking over all guards.

(d) 1 Coy 12th R.I.Rifles, 1 Coy 9th London Regt and 2 Platoons 6th London Regt. will proceed by lorry to the new area at 13.00 hours on July 8th taking over guards on July 9th under arrangements to be made direct by Commanding Officers concerned. Guides will be available at 2nd Lowland Brigade H.Qrs on July 8th if required.
Dress - Marching Order. Lewis Guns and 8 drums per gun will be taken on the lorry.

(e) All Defence Schemes, Regulations and orders as to Frontier Posts and Civil Administration and details as to training facilities will be taken over on relief.

7. The Guard over the Ammunition Train at ROMMERSKIRCHEN Station at present found by 12th R.I.Rifles will be relieved by 2nd Lowland Bde. Tents, rations, water, etc., will be handed over on relief.
Details will be issued later.

8. The Civil Staff Captain and P.R.O. and Staff will move with the Brigade Group taking over the administration of the new area at 16.00 hours on July 9th.
The P.R.O. will hand over all Orders re Civil Administration and hutting impovement schemes in the present area to the 2nd Lowland Bde.

-3-

9. All Defence Schemes in case of Civil Disturbances in the present area and orders re motor control at night (vide IV Corps R.O. 28 of 26/4/19) will be handed over on relief.

10. Separate administrative instructions will be issued.

11. All maps of a scale of 1/25,000 of the present area will be handed over on relief. Maps of this scale and 1/50,000 will be taken over by advance parties of the Brigade from units they are relieving.

12. All billets, guardrooms, stores etc., will be left clean. Schemes for combating the fly nuisance will be handed over.

13. Completion of moves and relief of guards will be reported to Brigade Headquarters.

14. 2nd Light Brigade Headquarters will close at GILL at 12.00 hours on July 9th and open at the same hour at 89 WEYER OHLIGS.

15. ACKNOWLEDGE.

G. Whittuck,
Captain,
Brigade Major.
2nd Light Brigade.

Issued at   hours.

Copy No. 1 to 12th R.I.Rifles.
         2 to 6th London Regt.
         3   9th London Regt.
         4   2nd Machine Gun Battn.
         5   2nd Light T.M. Battery.
         6   483rd Field Coy R.E.
         7   No 2 Coy. Train.
         8   Civil Staff Captain.
         9   Light Division.
         10   Light Division "Q".
         11   1st Light Brigade.
         12   2nd Light Brigade.
         13   Brigade Supply Officer.
         14   Light Divisional Train.
   15 & 16   2nd Lowland Brigade.
         17. G. O. C.
         18. Staff Captain.
         19   Brigade Signalling Officer.
   20 & 21   War Diary.
         22   File.

12th. R.I.Rifles.
6th. London Regt.
9th. London Regt.
2nd. Light T.M.B.
Detachment, 483rd.Field Coy.R.E.
No.2 Coy.Train.
Capt.ELLIOTT.
Civil Staff Captain,
P.R.O.
Brigade Q.M.S.
Brigade Transport Sergt.

2nd.Light Brigade

Ref.No.A.20/5/2.

Reference 2nd.Light Brigade Order No.3. and A.20/5 and A.20/5/1.

1. SUPPLIES.

Supply Railhead changes to OHLIGS on 11th.instant.

2. ADVANCE PARTIES.

(Reference A.20/5, para.4.)

Lorries taking advance parties from units of this Brigade will not bring back advance parties of corresponding units of 2nd. Lowland Division. The latter will be conveyed to this area under Lowland Division arrangements.

3. EXTRA TRANSPORT

(Reference A.20/5, para.2.)

Lorries as under are allotted for the conveyance of stores from billets to the entraining station, and from the detraining station to billets. The former will report to units at 07.00 hours, 9th.instant, and return to M.T.Coy. BEDBURG, on completion of duty. The latter will report at the detraining station on arrival of trains.

	Entraining.	Detraining.
Brigade Headquarters.	1	1
12th.R.I.Rifles.	5	4
6th.London Regt.	4	4
9th.London Regt.	5	4
2nd.Light T.M.B.	1	1
483rd. Field Coy.R.E.	1	1

On arrival at the detraining station, each unit will detail one representative to take over the lorries allotted to it from Staff Captain or N.C.O. i/c Lorries.

4. LORRIES FOR RELIEFS.

(Reference Para.6. Order No.3.)

Lorries will be allotted as under:-

Unit.	Date.	Time.	All ranks.	Head of Column.
12th.R.I.R.	8th.July.	13.00 hrs.	150.	STOMMELN on STOMMELN-COLOGNE road facing COLOGNE.
6th.London Regt.	-do-	13.00 "	60	South end of BUTZHEIM on BERGHEIM-ANSTEL road, facing South.
9th.London Regt.	-do-	13.00 "	150	NIEDERAUSSEM on NIEDERAUSSEM-ROMMERSKIRCHEN road, facing North.

5. ENTRAINING.

    (a) All units of this Brigade entrain at ROMMERSKIRCHEN and detrain at OHLIGS.

    (b) The time of entrainment is not yet known.

    (c) Two personnel trains and two transport trains are allotted for the conveyance of this Brigade. These are composed as under:-

    Each personnel train   2 coaches - (each 22 to 25 Officers)
                                      48 covers - (each 30 to 35 men)

    Each transport train   1 coach   - (22 to 25 Officers)
                                     17 flats   - (4 axles per flat)
                                     30 covers - (each 30 to 35 men or 8 L.D. or 6 H.D. or 10 to 15 tons baggage.)

Owing to short time allowed for loading personnel trains, all baggage should be sent on transport trains.

    (d) Trains will be made up as follows:-

    A. 1st.PERSONNEL TRAIN.

Unit.	Approx.strength.	Entraining Offrs.
Brigade H.Q.	1 Offr. 140 O.R's.	12th.R.I.R. will detail a senior Officer to conduct, in conjunction with R.T.O., entraining of all these units. Each unit, will, in addition detail one Officer to conduct entraining of own unit under orders of above senior officer, 12th.R.I.R. and R.T.O.,
12th.R.I.R.	40 " 500 "	
2nd.L.T.M.B.	2 " 32 "	
Det.483rd.R.E.	1 " 30 "	
No.2 Coy.Train.	3 " 66 "	

PTO

B. 2nd. PERSONNEL TRAIN.

Unit.	Approx. strength.	Entraining Officers.
6th. London Rgt.	23 Offrs. 500 O.R's	9th. London Regt. will detail a senior officer to conduct, in conjunction with R.T.O. entraining of both units. Unit entraining Officers as above.
9th. London Rgt.	27 " 500 "	

C. 1st. TRANSPORT TRAIN.

Unit.	Stores. No. of covers allotted for	Entraining Officers.
Brigade H.Q.	1.	12th. R.I. Rifles will detail one officer to be in command of this train and to act as entraining Officer.
12th. R.I. Rifles.	2.	
No. 2 Coy. Train.	Nil.	
Det. 483rd. Field Coy. RE.	1.	

D. 2nd. TRANSPORT TRAIN.

Unit.	No. of trucks allotted for stores.	Entraining Officer
6th. London Regt.	3	6th. London Regt. will detail one officer as for "C" train.
9th. London Regt.	3	
2nd. L.T.M.B.	1	

E. Entraining Officers of "C" and "D" trains will ensure that only transport laid down in this office No.A.20/5/1 of to-day's date is allowed to entrain. Transport on each train must be entrained as a whole and not by units, as the number of flats allotted will not allow of a sub-allotment to units.

F. On Train "C", 12th. R.I. Rifles will provide loading party for whole train. On Train "D", 6th. and 9th. London Regiments will each detail their own loading parties. Loading party of 12th. R.I. Rifles will not exceed 100 men. Loading parties of 6th. and 9th. London Regiments will not exceed 50 men each.

G. Entraining Officers will report to R.T.O. in advance of units. Times of reporting will be notified as soon as

-4-

        times of trains and times allowed for loading are known. Each unit entraining Officer will hand to the senior entraining Officer entraining strengths on the attached form. The senior entraining Officer, after taking what information he requires, will hand these over to the R.T.O., Entraining strengths will be made out by trains.

        Copies of entraining strengths will be forwarded to this office.

    H.   Units will not enter the station-yard until ordered to do so by the R.T.O., or entraining Officer. Care must be taken, however, that roads are kept clear.

    I.   Units will provide own ropes for fastening horses.

    J.   Entraining Officers will supervise detraining.

    K.   P.R.O. will make necessary traffic control arrangements at the station in consultation with R.T.O.

6. **D.A.D.O.S.**

    D.A.D.O.S. will close at LIPP on July 10th. and open at OHLIGS K.8547. on July 11th.

7. **CANTEEN.**

    The Canteen will close at BEDBURG on July 8th. and open at 68 COLNER STRASSE, OHLIGS, on July 10th.

8. **LAUNDRY.**

    The Laundry will close at BEDBURG on July 9th. and open at the School, DUNCANKENBURGEN Strasse, OHLIGS, on July 11th.

9. **RECEPTION CAMP.**

    The Reception Camp will close at FRAUWEILER on July 10th. and open the same day at KEIZER Hotel (opposite station) OHLIGS.

10. Acknowledge.

                                    Captain,
                              Staff Captain,
7/7/19.   2nd. Light Brigade.

Copies for G.O.C.,
          B.M.,

12th. R.I.Rifles.
8th. London Regt.
9th. London Regt.
2nd. Light T.M.B.
No.2 Coy.Train.
Det. 483rd.Field Coy.R.E.
Brigade Major,
Education Officer,-
Civil Staff Captain,
Brigade Q.M.S.
2nd.Lowland Brigade.

2nd.Light Brigade

Ref.No.A.80/6.

Reference 2nd.Light Brigade Order No.3. dated 6th.July.

1. **SUPPLIES.**

   There will be a double refilling on the 8th.instant, and not on 7th. as already ordered.

   The first refilling will be done by 1st.Line Transport, and the second by supply wagons, the latter then remaining with units until the completion of the move.

   Units will, therefore, move with rations for consumption for the day of move on the men and on the cookers, and rations for the day after the move on the supply wagons. Supply wagons will move with units, but will rejoin No.2 Coy.Train on completion of the move and after dumping supplies.

   Refilling point in the new area will be at MARKET STRASSE, OHLIGS. Commencing 9th.instant, and until further orders, rations will be drawn by 1st.Line Transport from MARKET STRASSE, OHLIGS, at 10.00 hours daily.

2. **EXTRA TRANSPORT FOR STORES.**

   The number of lorries allotted for the conveyance of surplus stores will be notified as soon as known.

3. **TRAIN ARRANGEMENTS.**

   Will be notified as soon as known.

4. **ADVANCE PARTIES.**

   Lorries for advance parties will report as under on the day previous to the move:-

Unit.	No.of lorries.	Place.	Time of reporting.
12th.R.I.Rifles,	1 lorry	STOMMELN.	06.00 hours.
8th.London Regt,	1 "	NETTESHEIM.	-do-
9th.London Regt,	1 "	NIEDERAUSSEM.	-do-
Remainder of * Brigade Group, Less 2nd.M.G.Bn,	1 "	Brigade H.Qrs. GILL.	-do-

   * Billeting parties from those units, as under, will pick up the lorry at Brigade Headquarters.

   2nd.L.T.M.B.   1 Offr, 1 O.R.
   No.2 Coy.Train.   3 All ranks.
   Brigade Headquarters, remainder of accommodation with personnel to take over Brigade Headquarters, Signal Exchanges, baths, etc.,

   The lorries taking advance parties from units of this Brigade will bring back advance parties of corresponding

PTO

-2-

units of the 2nd. Lowland Brigade.

5. BATHS.

Baths are located as follows, and will be taken over as under:-

   (a) 2nd. Lowland Brigade School. To be taken over by 12th. Royal Irish Rifles.
   (b) HUID STRASSE SCHOOL, WALD.   " "   " " " Brigade H.Qrs. for Use of Brigade H.Qrs. 9th. London Reg 2nd. L.T.M.B. 485rd. Field Co R.E.
   (c) ERNE FACTORY, WALD.   " "   " " " 9th. London Rgt (at present under repair)
   (d) School in ALTENHOVER STRASSE, WALD. " "   " " "
      ORR Disinfector " "   " " " 8th. London Rgt

In addition to the baths at 2nd. Lowland Brigade School, 12th. R.I. Rifles will take over all accommodation of the school.

Baths (b), (c) and (d) above will be taken over from 2nd. Lowland Brigade Headquarters.

6. BARRACK AND CAMP STORES.

No Camp, Barrack or area stores will be taken to new area, but handed over to incoming units. (e.g. beds, paillasses, tents, latrines, latrine buckets, meat safes, ablution benches, soyer stoves, rifle racks, etc.,)

Plates and cups will not be handed over.

Receipts will be obtained for all stores handed over and duplicates forwarded to this office, together with duplicate receipts for stores taken over in new area.

                                                  Captain,
                                          Staff Captain,
ly, 1919.   2nd. Light Brigade.

SECRET.

To:- 12th Battn. R.I.Rifles.   2nd Light Brigade. O.F./5.
    6th Battn. London Regt.
    9th Battn. London Regt.
    2nd Machine Gun Battn.
    2nd Light T.M. Battery.
    483rd Field Coy. R.E.
    No 2 Company Train.
    18th K. R. R. C.
    6th Field Ambulance.
    Civil Staff Captain.
    Light Division.   )
    Light Division Q.   ) for information.

---

1. In the event of the Division being ordered to move back to its normal area, the following warning instructions are issued.

2. On the day the order is received (A-1 Day) if not too late in the evening, one Battalion from each Infantry Brigade of the Northern Division will move by bus to COLOGNE.
   On A Day guards found by 9th London Regt. and 18th K. R. R. C. will be relieved by "A" Battalion 1st Northern Bde.
   Guards found by 6th London Regt by "A" Battalion 2nd Northern Brigade.
   Guards found by 12th R.I.Rifles by "A" Battalion 3rd Northern Brigade.

3. On B Day the Brigade Group will proceed to GILL Area by bus.
   The times and places of embussing will probably be as follows :-

   09.00 hours. 6th London Regt. PIUS STRASSE. head   27 busses)
                                  facing E at junction of   )
                                  VENLOER & PIUS STRASSE.   )
   09.00 hours. 9th London Regt. EIFEL Infantry Barracks
                                  facing North.   30   "
   14.00 hours. 12th R.I.Rifles.   do   33   "
        do   (Bde H.Qrs & 2nd
                 (Light T. M. B.   do   6   "
        do   1 Section 483rd
                  Field Coy. R.E.   do   2   "
        do   6th London Regt. do   2   "
        do   9th London Regt. do   2   "

   Lorries will be provided for stores. Dress - Marching Order. Lewis Guns and 8 drums per Gun will be carried on busses.

4. Should the order be received so late on A-1 Day that it is not possible for advanced Battalions of Northern Division to move into COLOGNE, relief of guards will take place on B Day and the move back to normal areas on C Day.

5. Transport will proceed direct by road. There will be no staging. Distances will be maintained on the march in accordance with S.S.C. pamphlet on March Discipline. Times for march will be issued later.

-2-

6.   18th K. R. R. C. will proceed by boat to normal area, embarking near SUD Bridge on E Day (C Day if relief of guards is postponed).

7.   2nd Machine Gun Battn. will proceed to its normal area under orders received from Light Division.

8.   Please acknowledge.

24/6/19.

Captain.
Brigade Major.
2nd Light Brigade.

Army Form C. 2118.

WAR DIARY – AUGUST. 1919.

INTELLIGENCE SUMMARY.

(Erase heading not required).

Instructions regarding War Diaries and Intelligence Summaries are contained in F.S. Regs., Part II. and the Staff Manual respectively. Title pages will be prepared in manuscript.

Place	Date	Hour	Summary of Events and Information	Remarks and references to Appendices
	1.		6th.Bn.London Regiment firing G.M.C. Other Training normal. 12th.R.I.Rifles held Eliminating Battn.Sports.	
	2.		Training as above. 6th.London Regt. Eliminating Sports.	
	3.		Training as above. 12th.R.I.Rifles and 6th.London Regt. held Eliminating Sports.	
	4.		General Holiday.	
	5–7.		Training as above. On the 7th. 12th.R.I.Rifles. held Battalion Sports.	
	8.		2nd.Class Army Certificate Examination held in all Units.	
	9.		3rd.Class Army Certificate Examination held in all Units.	
	10–13.		Training normal.	
	14.		War Office representative from S.D.8. visited Brigade and inspected Handyman Training in the workshops of the 12th.R.I.Rifles.	
	15.		Brigade Sports. Winners 9th.London Regt.	
	16–17.		Training normal.	
	18.		Brigade Boxing Competition. Winners 12th.R.I.Rifles.	
	19.		6th.Bn. London Regt. finish G.M.C.	
	20.		Brigade Cross-Country Race. Winners 9th.London Regt. Brigade Basket-Ball Competition. Winners 12th.R.I.Rifles. The Brigade Championship Cup presented by Brigadier-General R.A.M.CURRIE. CMG. DSO. was won by the 12th.R.I.Rifles.	

PTO

Army Form C. 2118.

WAR DIARY – AUGUST, 1919.

INTELLIGENCE SUMMARY.

(Erase heading not required.)

Instructions regarding War Diaries and Intelligence Summaries are contained in F. S. Regs., Part II. and the Staff Manual respectively. Title pages will be prepared in manuscript.

Place	Date	Hour	Summary of Events and Information	Remarks and references to Appendices
	21.		1 Company, 9th.Bn. London Regt. relieved 1 Company, 12th.R.I.Rifles, in left sub-section of Outpost Line.	
	22.		12th.Bn. 12th. R.I.Rifles commenced firing G.M.G.	
	23-31		Training normal. The 12th.R.I.Rifles have the range at their disposal. On the 22nd. Lieut.-Colonel E.B.POWELL. DSO. assumed command of the 6th.Bn. London Regiment: Lieut.-Colonel J.B.BRADY. DSO. being posted to the 18th.Bn. K.R.R.C.	

6/9/19.

[signature]
for Brigadier General,
Commanding 2nd.Light Brigade.

Army Form C. 2118.

WAR DIARY
or
INTELLIGENCE SUMMARY
(Erase heading not required.)

OCTOBER 1919

Instructions regarding War Diaries and Intelligence Summaries are contained in F.S. Regs. Part II. and the Staff Manual respectively. Title pages will be prepared in manuscript.

Place	Date	Hour	Summary of Events and Information	Remarks and references to Appendices
OHLIGS.	1 - 8		Training proceeded normally. 9th London Regiment firing General Musketry Course.	
	9		Brigadier General R. A. M. CURRIE, C.M.G., D.S.O., proceeded to United Kingdom on leave. Lieut. Colonel GOODWIN, C.M.G., D.S.O., 12th Royal Irish Rifles assumed Command 2nd Light Brigade.	
			Education Officer proceeded to COLOGNE for three days visit to G.H.Q., General and Commercial College and Educational Conference.	
	10-11		Normal. Order sick received to be relief of a horse of his Outpost line north of HAAN by his Relgans. This relief was subsequently postponed indefinitely.	
	12		winter time adopted.	
	13-19		Normal demobilization of personnel now speeding up. By the 19th all horses in the Brigade, except eight, had been called in.	
	20		All Units sent vehicles and mobilization stores with Guards to Divisional Dump OHLIGS. All surplus stores handed in to D.A.D.O.S.	
	21		Normal.	
	22		6th London Regiment reduced to Cadre and moved to MERSCHEID. All retainable personnel sent to 15th and 18th K.R.R.C. 12th Royal Irish Rifles relieved in Outpost Line by 18th K.R.R.C. who moved to OHLIGS-WALD-HAAN Area. The Brigade area now administered by 1st Light Brigade.	
	23		12th Royal Irish Rifles left the Brigade and entrained at HAAN for the OPLADEN Area.	
	24		9th London Regiment reduced to Cadre, all retainable men sent to 15th and 20th K.R.R.C.	
	25		Brigadier General R.A.M. CURRIE, C.M.G., D.S.O., returned and assumed Command of the Brigade.	
			Strength: 11 Officers 93 Other Ranks.	

G. Whitlock Ryans
for Brigadier General,
Commanding 2nd Light Brigade.

		2nd Light Brigade.
12th Royal I. Rifles.	Light Division 'G'	
6th London Regiment.	Light Division 'Q'	
9th London Regiment.	3rd Light Brigade.	S E C R E T. Copy No. 15
2nd L.T.M. Battery.	Civil Staff Captain	
C.R.E., Light Division.	(No. 2 Sub-Area).	
6th Field Ambulance.	P.R.O. No. 2 Sub-Area.	
No. 2 Company Train.	Staff Captain.	

2nd Light Brigade Order No. O.P. 12/5.

1. On the 15th October the Belgian Army is to take over the 3rd Light Brigade Area and the area round HAAN as defined in 2nd Light Brigade Mis. 121 dated 11/10/19. (Issued to Units of the 2nd Light Brigade Group only).

   HOHE Post will remain inclusive to the Light Division.
   The troops of the Light Division in the area to be handed over will be relieved by the 171st French Regiment of the 77th French Division.

2. On the afternoon of 14th October two sections of the 171st French Regiment are to relieve 1 Company, 12th Royal Irish Rifles holding Perimeter Posts LOOP to MANNERTMUHLE inclusive under arrangements made between Commanding Officers concerned. If necessary a proportion of Officers and N.C.O's will be left at the Posts by 12th Royal I. Rifles for 48 hours after relief.
   On relief 1 Company, 12th Royal I. Rifles will move to HAAN.

3. Guides will be provided by 12th Royal I. Rifles to be at the FERRY HIMMELGEIST by 1300 hours October 14th as follows :-

   (a) One French speaking Officer to guide H.Q. of Company and one Section to HAAN.

   (b) One N.C.O. from each Post to guide relieving Units.

4. French troops will reach HAAN about 1600 hours on October 14th by tra   under arrangements being made by 3rd Light Brigade.

5. On October 15th 12th Royal I. Rifles will move to OHLIGS by march route clearing HAAN by 1000 hours and will be accommodated West of the OHLIGS - HAAN Railway. No restrictions as to route. Distances will be maintained on the march as in para. 1 'Notes on March Discipline'. The necessary adjustments in accommodation in OHLIGS will be made by 6th London Regiment by 1800 hours October 14th.

6. 12th Royal I. Rifles and 6th London Regiment will provide an Officer each to meet a representative from the Civil Staff Captain in OHLIGS to arrange Officers' accommodation etc. on the morning of October 14th. Time and place will notified later to Units direct by the Civil Staff Captain.

7. The 77th French Division will take over the Civil Administration of HAAN on October 15th. Further instructions will be issued later.

8. All defence schemes, information as to training areas, ranges etc., will be handed over on relief and receipts obtained. The BRUCKER-KOTTEN Rifle Range will not be handed over.

9. Instructions as to the handing over of the area stores and the provision of lorries for moving stores will be issued separately.

10. Completion will be reported to Brigade Headquarters.

11. ACKNOWLEDGE.

13/10/19.

A. Whittuck.
Brigade Major, 2nd Light Captain, Brigade.

To:- All recipients of O.O.12/8/1.   2nd Light Brigade No.O.O.12/8/2

SECRET.

1. Reference para. 3 of O.O.12/8/1 dated 20/10/19, 12th R. I. Rifles will move to OPLADEN on October 22nd probably by road.

Detailed orders will be issued later.

One Company 18th K.R.R.C. will not now move to WALD but direct to HAAN and relieve the perimeter posts of 12th R. I. Rifles with two platoons on October 22nd.

Relief of perimeter posts to be complete by 12 noon. All other details will be arranged between Commanding Officers concerned.

2. Reference para. 2 of O.O.12/8/1, 18th K.R.R.C. will probably move 1 Company to the STRASSENBAHN, WALD.

Captain,
Brigade Major,
2nd Light Brigade.

20/10/19.

12th Royal I. Rifles.	1st Light Brigade.	2nd Light Brigade.
6th London Regiment.	Staff Captain.	
9th London Regiment.	Brigade Supply Officer.	No. O.P.12/6/1.
2nd L. T. M. Battery.	Civil Staff Captain.	
C.R.E.	P.R.O. No. 2 Sub-Area.	S E C R E T.
No. 2 Company Train.	Light Division.	
6th Field Ambulance.	Light Division "Q".	

1. The reduction to Cadre of 6th and 9th London Regiments and the cross-posting of retainable Officers and other ranks of these Battalions to the 1st Light Brigade will commence on Wednesday, October 22nd, moves taking place in accordance with a table to be issued later and will be completed by October 25th.
Retainable personnel of 6th London Regiment for Units of 1st Light Brigade other than 18th K.R.R.C. will move to SOLINGEN on October 22nd, retainable personnel of 9th London Regiment to 1st Light Brigade on October 24th.

2. This re-organisation necessitates the move of 18th K.R.R.C. less one Company of the 1st Light Brigade to OHLIGS on October 23rd.

3. It is probable that the 12th Royal I. Rifles will be ordered to move from HAAN to OPLADEN at an early date as a Garrison for the latter place.
If this move takes place, the 12th Royal I. Rifles will be relieved by one Company of 18th K.R.R.C. of the 1st Light Brigade, disposed as follows-

    1 Company (less two platoons) HAAN.

    2 Platoons holding Perimeter Posts MANNERTMUHLE to LOOP inclusive at present occupied by one Company 12th Royal I. Rifles.

    1 Company 18th K.R.R.C. moves to STRANDBATHS, WALD on October 23rd in preparation for this relief.

4. AT 1400 hours on October 23rd Command of the present 2nd Light Light Brigade Area passes to G.O.C. 1st Light Brigade.

5(a) 2nd Light Brigade Headquarters will continue to remain at WEYER till further orders and administer the Cadres of the 6th and 9th London Regiments. In the event of civil disturbances Cadres of 6th and 9th London Regiments will be at the disposal of the G.O.C. 1st Light Brigade.
 (b) The Civil Administration of the present Brigade Area passes to G.O.C 1st Light Brigade at 1400 hours on October 23rd. The Civil Administrative and P.R.O's Staff will remain at WALD until further orders under the 1st Light Brigade.

6. Cadres of 6th and 9th London Regiments will be concentrated and disposed as follows:-

    6th London Regiment   OHLIGS. east of IHLIGS-HAAN Rly.

    9th London Regiment   WALD. ALTEN MOVER STRASSE and S of the WALD-CENTRAL Road.

7. The Cadre of 2nd Light T. M. Battery will be attached to the 9th London Regiment on a date to be notified later.

8. Orders as to disposal of Maps, Musketry Stores, etc., will be issued later.

9. ACKNOWLEDGE.

Captain,

Royal I. Rifles;   1st Light Brigade.
London Regiment;   Staff Captain;
London Regiment;   Brigade Supply Officer;
T. M. Battery;   Civil Staff Captain;
                        P.R.O. No. 2 Sub-Area;   2nd Light Brigade.
Company Train;   Light Division;
Field Ambulance;   Light Division "Q".   No. O.P. 12/6/3.
                                                         S E C R E T.

Reference para. 3 of O.P.12/6/1 dated 20/10/19.

1(a). The 12th Royal I. Rifles (less transport) will move to OPLADEN to on October 23rd.
Arrangements may be made by O.C. 12th Royal I. Rifles to send a portion of the Battalion by train provided that not more than 25 men proceed on any one train. The remainder of the Battalion will proceed by march rout via LANGENFELD, clearing HAAN by 1000 hours. The tram may be used from LANGENFELD provided that formed parties only proceed by tram.
Billets will be obtained from the Town Major at OPLADEN to whom advanced parties should be sent to report by 0900 hours on October 23rd.

(b) Six lorries have been applied for for the transport of baggage (including mobile reserve S.A.A., packs, steel helmets and box respirators).

(c) A Guard of 1 Officer and 8 Other Ranks will be left in charge of equipment stored at OHLIGS rationed by Divisional Train. All Lewis Guns except those issued for instructional purposes, will be retained with the Battalion and not stored with other equipment at OHLIGS.

(d) On arrival at OPLADEN the 12th Royal I. Rifles will come under the direct orders of Light Divisional Headquarters for all purposes (i.e. tactical and administrative). Official correspondence will be addressed direct to Light Divisional Headquarters.

J. Whittuck,
Captain,
Brigade Major,
2nd Light Brigade.

21/10/19.

2nd Light Brigade No. O.P.12/6/4.

21. X. 19.

Moves in connection with reduction of 6th and 9th London Regiments.

(Reference 2nd Light Brigade No. O.P.12/6/1 dated 20/10/19)

Date.	Unit.	From.	To.	Time of starting.	Route.	Remarks.
Oct. 22nd.	6th London. Retainable.	OHLIGS.	13th K.R.R.C. H.Q., Kaiser Strasse, SOLINGEN.	1330 hours.	MERSCHEID - SOLINGEN.	6th and 9th London Regiments will arrange to give dinners to their men before the move. Tea ration will be sent in advance by Battalions to which men are being posted.
Oct. 23rd.	do	Present area.	18th K.R.R.C.	To be complete by 1600 hours.	—	Exact numbers of Officers and Other Ranks for cross-posting will be detailed later.
Oct. 23rd.	6th London Cadre.	do	East of OHLIGS- HAAN Railway.	To be complete by 1200 hours.	—	
	9th London Cadre.	Concentrate around ALTENHOVEN Strasse, WALD.		To be complete by 1000 hours.	—	
Oct. 24th.	9th London Retainable.	WALD.	13th K.R.R.C. H.Q. Kaiser Strasse, SOLINGEN. 20th K.R.R.C. H.Q. Schwert Strasse, Solingen.	1330 hours.	CENTRAL - SOLINGEN.	
	2nd L.T.M.Bty.	WALD. (attd 9th Londons).	1st Light T.M.B. Schule Str. SOLINGEN.	do	do	

Captain,
for Brigade Major,
2nd Light Brigade.

www.ingramcontent.com/pod-product-compliance
Lightning Source LLC
Chambersburg PA
CBHW081454160426
43193CB00013B/2480